*THE DESPERATION OF A WOMAN:
LESSONS ABOUT LIVING AND LOVING*

Monekka L. Munroe

The Desperation of a Woman

Copyright © 2013
Monekka L. Munroe

All rights reserved. No part of this book may be reproduced in any form without the expressed written permission of the publisher, except by a reviewer.

Great Minds Publishing
P.O. Box 5795
Tallahassee, Fl 32314

greatmindspublishing@gmail.com

Printed in USA
First Printing in 2011

ISBN-10: 0989005003
ISBN-13: 978-0-9890050-0-5

This book is dedicated to my friend, my angel, the source of my strength and my lifeline. This book is for my daughter, Aariel. May life give to you its all, as I am sure you will give to it the same.

Special Acknowledgements

So many people remained patient with me throughout this process. However, I wish to first give all praises to the Creator who remains so merciful, loving and forgiving. Thank you for instilling in me the spirit to love and give back to my community unselfishly. I want to recognize everyone who continuously called to encourage me to keep writing and typing, especially those times I was on the verge of giving up. I also want to say a special thank you to those who not only asked about the completion of the book, but also asked how you could help. Every one of you played such a significant role in the birth of The Desperation of a Woman. Whether your part was small or large, without you, this book would not have come to fruition. For that, I thank you all.

Contents

Message to the Black Woman   7

Introduction

    It's O.K.   8

Chapter One

    Friendship   11

Chapter Two

    Women with Children   20

Chapter Three

    Educated Women   52

Chapter Four

    Married Women   66

Chapter Five

Remembering Our Elders	78
Epilogue	83
Appendix-A	86
Appendix-B	89

Women, no longer can we ignore the fact that we are just as responsible for much of the destruction that we have in our homes and in our lives.

Today we will start over. Today we will nurture our minds, embrace our differences, take better care of ourselves and our children. We will begin to understand the struggles of all Black men and make every attempt to love and support them along with applauding their efforts of survival.

Yesterday we were in pain. Today we will begin the healing process. Tomorrow we will love.

mlm

INTRODUCTION

It's o.k.

Being alone can be an awakening experience, only if you're ready to face the truth about yourself. When some women are alone they are faced with nothing except themselves, their fears, and their demons. For many women this is a painful task; the loneliness forces them to confront those fears and demons. As a result of this confrontation, women will either fight to gain wisdom and strength or avoid those fears and demons altogether by participating in destructive behaviors such as abusing drugs, abusing their bodies, abusing others and/or becoming involved in unhealthy relationships.

For some, it is easier to become involved in relationships and attempt to solve the problems of others, in doing so, the woman can continue avoiding her own demons. These women quickly become "relationship evangelists"; they give advice to friends about relationship issues, while unwilling to follow their own advice.

As women, we are very peculiar beings when facing the truth about ourselves. Often a "friend" will scold us for dating a man who treats us less than the queens we are. The "friend" will quickly say, "You should have left his sorry ass a long time ago." She will go on to say that she "would never put up wit no #*# like that." However, she often forgets about the hidden bruises she has because of her abusive boyfriend/husband. Yet she has the audacity to admonish someone else for the choices they've made in their relationship!

A mirror can be the most powerful item in a woman's home. We look in the mirror several times before leaving our home and we look in the mirror before inviting others into our home. This piece of glass shows us what looks appealing and what should be altered before someone else sees us. We trust this piece of glass before we trust ourselves.

Just when we think our makeup is flawless, our hair is fried, dyed, and laid to the side, we look in the mirror and discover that something needs to be changed. Based on the reflection in a piece of glass, we are late for school, church, and late for work. If it were possible, some of us would be late for our own funeral based on what we see in the mirror. This mirror concept is just one example of how women often look to other sources for validation. We look in the mirror to clarify that we look acceptable to the outside world.

There are also times when we ask others much too quickly for their opinion about our lives, our choices, and our decisions. We look to many external sources for validation they cannot provide.

Some of our external characteristics are the result of internal pain. We know the struggles of our daily existence; we are the only ones who can soothe and ultimately heal ourselves of those struggles.

Once this healing process begins, we can then begin to look internally for validation of who we are. We can now accept the fact that we aren't perfect, we have flaws, we have lied and deceived, we have cheated at something or on someone, and we have caused someone pain. Once these facts are realized, we can start to love ourselves, and stop waiting for something or someone to tell us that we're worth being loved. Let us begin.

Chapter One

Friendship

> "Don't allow your trash to become someone's treasure."
>
> -author

For most of us, our mother is the first woman with whom we have a personal relationship. Did she talk about self-love and exploring the beauty of self? What life lessons did your mother teach about other women and friendship?

Why do so many women have difficulty developing and maintaining friendships with other women? Why do some women prefer to befriend a male instead of a female?

Some women feel issues such as trust and competition thwart healthy female friendships. Others described the betrayal by best friends who had sexual relationships with their boyfriends or husbands. One woman stated, "I just have a natural distrust of other women."

So, where does the initial mistrust come from? Have we all had negative experiences with women in the past?

Is it possible that we began our mistrust of women from unhealthy relationships with our mother? Is our definition of friendship distorted or could it be that we never learned how to be a friend?

Some women prefer to have more male than female friends. If this is true, why do so many women continue dating men who weren't created for them? We should have obtained a plethora of knowledge about men because of these male "friendships."

Although there are several reasons women do not maintain healthy friendships with one another, this chapter will discuss three of the most common reasons—baggage, men, and loyalty.

Some women carry a lot of baggage, and at times unaware, it is weighing them down. It (baggage) can be defined as childhood traumas, mental, physical and sexual abuse, unsuccessful adult relationships, loneliness, abandonment and neglect. This baggage causes them to engage in unhealthy friendships with women and men. It can also cause low self-esteem, anger, and feelings of envy toward other women.

I think at some point in our lives, we've not only met this bag lady, but we were that lady. When discussing men, she constantly tells or asks about the man in your life.

She will attempt to give dumb advice such as, "He ain't for you and you deserve better." However, keep in mind she doesn't have a man! If she does have one, she is so caught up with your business, she has lost track of her own. She has completely forgotten about her own family; she brings the problems of her friends to the dinner table instead of asking about her children's academic progress and she shares these problems while in her bedroom instead of making love to her significant other. She knows everything about everybody except herself.

Baggage can also blind us from seeing the realities of life. As long as we continue to hold on to past hurt, we're unable to see how beautiful we truly are, and we become oblivious to the love and support we can give to each other. Instead, we are jealous of those who experience any type of status change. That change includes marital or economic status, or even an education status (i.e. from Master's degree to Ph.D). It is even difficult at times to say hello with a genuine smile and give another woman a compliment, because of the hurt we refuse to let go.

If you're constantly experiencing problems in your personal relationships, and other arenas, maybe you've allowed your baggage to weigh you down and cause you to become a bag lady.

We have all experienced our share of hurt but we must make it a priority to face the pain, forgive those who have hurt us, forgive ourselves for the hurt we may have caused, and move forward. The time has come to stop masking our pain and realize that although it is ok to hurt, it's also ok to live pain free. This can be accomplished by ending relationships and habits that can alter the path to mental freedom.

The second and most popular reason women cannot maintain healthy friendships is due to the one thing we just can't seem to survive without, men. Ladies, there are times when we have fallen in love much too quickly and totally lost ourselves because of the new man in our life.

Newfound love will cause us to stop speaking to almost everyone we know in an effort to show tremendous loyalty to a man who possibly doesn't love us in return. Love has caused fights and scandal in just about every environment that exists; some women have even fought in the church about their men. If this man has great sexual skills, this further weakens the mind of a woman and renders her helpless!

She will fight with her best friend, her mother, and at times, neglect her children about this man. During those times of turbulence, a true friend will be there always.

She will cry with you during the bad times and laugh with you during the good times. Some friends will be there just to offer advice and words of wisdom when needed. However, when a man is involved, those wise words are obsolete. The woman who believes she's in love will ignore warning signs from her friends, the man, and her own female intuition just to satisfy her hunger to be loved. The woman will even endure abuse, and lie to others in an effort to protect him, with the false belief the abuse will stop.

When a woman willingly gives this much of herself to a man, and has lost focus of everything and everyone around her, this is usually an indicator that her male suitor isn't much of a man. A good man, who is strong and confident in himself and in his relationship, doesn't require a woman to leave her family and friends just to be with him. In fact, most men admire women who can think for themselves and are able to show some level of independence.

Maybe, while we are analyzing the definition of friendship, we should also research the definition of a man.

One morning, while I sat on my porch, I watched as the sanitation workers collected the trash from each yard on my street.

It never occurred to me until that day how the specific duties of their job paralleled to so many other things in life. The broken trust of friendship is one of those situations. When that sacred bond is violated, an impenetrable wall is formed around the heart and mind of the betrayed friend. This is the third reason women cannot maintain friendships-loyalty.

Sharing our lives with friends, sometimes include sharing secrets (good/ bad) and other pieces of information in confidence. When talking with true friends, we feel very relaxed and self-assured knowing the information being shared will go no further than that moment. Well, at least that's how it should be; however, there are unfortunate times when we realize someone in our close circle is not a friend, but a common trash collector.

The trash collector will go from house to house gathering gossip and listening to the sorrows of her friends. She will then, take that gossip to anyone who will allow her to bring the garbage of other people's lives into their home. She will often pick through your garbage and choose what she feels is the most valuable pieces and use them to cause harm. She has manipulated the friendship and used your trash as her treasure.

Being cautious of this type of woman can prevent a lot of drama, however, we must also make sure we have not allowed ourselves to become a garbage dumping ground. The morning I sat watching the men collect the garbage, I wondered where they were taking it. Then it hit me, there is a place reserved just for garbage! Unloading trash is not acceptable everywhere, it has to be taken to a specific place, and all trash collectors know exactly where those places are! Women who are destined to cause doom, know exactly where to garner support for negativity, they will surround themselves with other negative women who are waiting to welcome them with open arms and ears.

We should not be a vessel for insult and hurt. There is something truly wrong when we find joy in hearing about the pain of others. We determine the type of conversation we choose to engage in. If you are in the company of these discussions, and you just sit quietly, you are a part of the problem. There may be times when you have to walk away, or change the subject by sharing some good news, or by saying something positive. Never the less, we never know when we will need someone to witness for us. So, why not be that vessel of goodness; speaking words to encourage your sisters instead of using words to tear them down?

I believe women can have long, healthy friendships with one another by accepting and caring for each other unconditionally, without limitation. Unconditional means celebrating our friend's accomplishments without feelings of jealousy, accepting their flaws without judging, and respecting their right to think on their own- even when this conflicts with our opinion.

Not all of our friends can play the same role in our lives. Not all information can be shared with all friends. Some friends cannot handle our truths, some cannot accept the wholeness of who we are, while other friends will embrace that wholeness.
We have to identify the reasons people are in our lives and accept their delicate roles. We also have to identify the reasons we allow people to stay in our lives. People are who they are, we can accept them or not, we do have a choice. That is one of the beauties of being an individual; a true friend will understand and respect that. Once we are able to accept these beautiful differences, we can have a true, long-lasting friendship with other women.

The roles women play are never ending. We are mothers, sisters, daughters, girlfriends, wives, friends, and everything else that is required to keep this world revolving. There are times when only another female will understand our pain.

There will be those times when only a strong woman can provide words of comfort by saying, "Be strong girl, this too shall pass."

It is unfortunate that so many women haven't had the opportunity to have a best friend to pray, laugh and cry with; to share secrets with; to have manicures and pedicures with. It is so hurtful to know that although women are the backbones of this universe, and we have contributed so much to the survival of our people, yet, we cannot name five women that we can <u>honestly</u> call a **FRIEND.**

If you are experiencing difficulties befriending other females, is it possible that you never learned how to be a friend?

Chapter Two

Women with Children

> *"The mother is the first teacher of the child. The message that she gives that child, is the message that child gives to the world."*
>
> -Malcolm X

The term single mother simply means an unwed female with children. This phrase (single mother) is echoed many times as if there's an automatic understanding of struggle and doom. This is most unfortunate because though raising children alone is tough, it doesn't signify a life of disaster.

Although being a single mother is a reality for many women, parenting alone, without the assistance of the father is the topic of this chapter. Some of the fathers are no longer in the home because of separation, divorce, death, incarceration, and some leave voluntarily. Some of these fathers are married to other women therefore, unable to live in the home of the child they've fathered. Many women are raising the children of someone else (family members, friends), some chose to adopt with the understanding they will be single mothers and some are raising their children without the father because their actions, attitudes and personality caused the man to leave the home.

Whatever the reason, the reality is the same, raising children is a hard task. This fact remains true even when there are two active parents in the home. Many mothers work extremely hard and are successful in their efforts of providing their children with the necessary tools for survival and success. However, this chapter is written primarily for the mothers who may have lost their way (intentionally or unintentionally) while trying to parent their children.

There are mothers who desperately need assistance but don't realize it. This assistance is not in the form of money, but in the form of community support, mental health treatment, and parenting skills. Everything we do and say as parents impact our children. This may not be apparent to us but it's true. The effects of misguidance are displayed everywhere the child goes. When children are misbehaving, the behavior is often blamed on bad parenting and unfortunately, at times (not every time) this statement is true.

The Father

Where is he? Does he want to be involved with you or his child? If not, leave him alone.

Try to talk with him about support for the child, if that doesn't work, talk with an attorney. Make sure you are taking this step for **THE CHILDREN**. Child support payments are just that-**<u>CHILD SUPPORT</u>**. We need to start doing better with these funds. Take care of the babies; stay out of the shopping malls, nail and hair salons.

Soliciting support from the father should not occur as an effort to punish him because he no longer wants a relationship with the mother. In these instances, the welfare of the children is no longer a concern; the mother is stuck on vengeance, especially if the man begins a relationship with someone else.

If the father is active in the life of his child both physically and financially, accept the fact that the relationship is over between the two of you and acknowledge the blessing that he is a supportive father. Even during the times his money may not be readily available, remember that in the life of a child, the presence of the father, is more powerful than the state of his finances.

On the other hand, once you you've realized he does not want a relationship with his child, let him go. If you couldn't make him love you, what makes you think you can make him love the children?

Don't cause problems for the new woman in his life by calling to tell her of his wrong doings. If he continues his unfaithful ways, eventually, she will find out. Don't call his job or his home, and don't make attempts to become best buddies with his friends. Don't show up at the places you know he frequents, stay away from his property, don't stalk him and don't talk negatively about him in the presence of the children. Cry through the night, pray for strength and guidance, scream if you have to and talk to your best friend until the both of you fall asleep.

Do whatever you have to do to deal with the pain, but don't think by making life miserable for him that you will feel better, you won't.

Never mistreat your children, especially the child who resembles his/her father. Some women will show less love and support to the child who resembles their father. That's just plain stupid! This is the time to remember that you chose the father of your child, your child didn't make that choice. As soon as your pain heals, talk with your children. Be honest and explain what is happening with your family. Reassure them they are not the cause of the absence of their father, make them understand they will continue to be loved and supported. Explain that the family unit will not fall apart because of one missing parent. And most important, although our children cannot see Him, please make them aware that their heavenly Father is and will always care for them. Introduce God early in the lives of children, don't wait until trouble surfaces. Life goes on and so must you.

Welfare

In the minds of some, welfare and the Black family seem to be synonymous. These benefits include money, food stamps, Medicaid, subsidized housing and childcare. The entire system of welfare is flawed; it does not embrace the importance of family. In most cases, the father is forbidden to reside in the home with his family, and at times, the mother has to reside in substandard housing.

Sisters have to find a way to leave this system behind! Seek the education and knowledge that will open the door of opportunity.

Face your weakness, don't be afraid to continue your education, stop telling yourself that you can't do better. Realize you have the power to end the cycle of welfare dependency. You have the right to break any cycle of ignorance, self-hatred and darkness.

Believe in yourself enough to want change. Become hungry for knowledge and success. When no one else is there to do so, encourage yourself to make a difference within yourself.

More important than anything else, start loving yourself and your children enough to want a better life, and go for it!

Know that independence is one of God's greatest gifts. However, it has to be nurtured and strengthened daily. This world has so much to give, but no one will open that door of opportunity. We must open it for ourselves and kick it down if necessary, but this can only be achieved by changing our way of thinking, leaving old habits behind, facing fears, moving forward, and embracing challenges.

From boys to men

Currently, we are preparing too many Black boys for the institution of prison instead of the institution of higher education. We should be preparing them to be fathers, protectors, business owners, educators, and community leaders who can continue to uplift others who look like them.

Is it possible for a single mother to raise a Black boy into a Black man? Yes, I believe a woman is more than capable, in fact, I believe it is easier than raising a girl to become a woman. The reason is, many women have become so focused on finding a man, they've never realized the importance of developing their own womanhood. As a result, it would be difficult teaching womanhood to little girls.

As women, we know a man should work, this lesson can be taught early to our boys. We know a man should not physically nor mentally abuse women, teach those lessons to our sons. We all desire a man who is intelligent, caring and responsible. Why not instill these important characteristics in our sons? Yes, a single mother can raise a boy to become an intelligent, hardworking, and honest man.

This is achieved by first dismissing the notion that being born a Black male is to be born with two strikes against him. Being born Black is not a curse. It is a blessing bestowed upon us by the Almighty and it should not be viewed as anything less. It is imperative to help the male child understand who he *really* is and the importance of maintaining his *true* identity throughout his life. Teach him that as a child, he is a boy who will one day grow to be a strong, independent and fearless man.

Don't be afraid to be a parent, set rules and guidelines. Give them chores to teach responsibility, young boys should not be taught to shy away from hard work and accountability. They should not be cuddled each time they cry because of a bump or bruise, and under no circumstances, excuse wrongdoings in an effort to protect them.

Once the boy becomes a man, his excuses will not shield him from facing the severe consequences of his actions.

Teach him about the injustices of the criminal justice system against males who looks like him, and show him examples of these injustices. Make him aware of the countless numbers of Black males who have died or who remain imprisoned in America's penal system.* **YOUR SON IS NO EXCEPTION.**

Monitor his friends and associates, set a curfew, and know where he is and what he's doing. Provide books and other reading material to enhance his intelligence, even show caution about the toys that are purchased. For young boys, we tend to buy games and toys that promote play and physical action instead of the promotion of higher-level thinking. This is a dangerous practice because most of our younger, Black, male millionaires are wealthy due to the games they play (NBA, NFL) and with their money they continue to buy toys (multiple cars, jewelry, etc).

Although there is nothing wrong with the profession of any sport, we tend to show full support of our boys while they are playing sports, but not show up to the parent-teacher meetings at

---

* See Appendix A

school. This is giving the message that academics are not as important as playing. As loving mothers, it is our job to make sure our boys understand they are capable of doing more than playing sports. Reading, studying, preparing to be an academic scholar can also provide a bright future. Education must be a priority!

Warn him about the dangers of being touched inappropriately by others (family members, friends, and strangers) and make sure he knows he can come to you if such a thing does occur. Make it mandatory that he does volunteer work. Allow him to join local social clubs affiliated with educational success as well as male growth and development. Contact church leaders and the local chapters of various fraternities to inquire about possible male rites of passage ceremonies. The goal is to make sure there is continuous contact with men who are stable and able to assist with guidance in the direction of becoming a man.

I commend the efforts of the brothers of Omega Psi Phi, Incorporated. These men have a proven track record of changing the lives of Black youth. They have scholarship and mentoring programs, talent showcases, back to school give-a-ways, and many other beneficial programs that continue to educate our boys about responsibility, respect for themselves and others.

The Fly Jock, Tom Joyner (an Omega man) has gone a few steps further. He provides scholarships to students who attend Historically Black Colleges and Universities (HBCU). He provides financial assistance to mothers and fathers during his weekly radio broadcasts, and he continuously advocates for families and children.

Teach about the appropriate ways converse with females. Teach the true meaning of respect and that he should always demand respect in return. Help him appreciate the importance of thinking for himself so that he will not become so quickly attracted to being a follower.

Don't allow him to use the excuse of not having a father in his life as an excuse to act foolish (commit crimes, drop out of high school, use/abuse drugs, etc). Our job is to provide our children with the proper tools and foundation on which to build.

Young boys need to understand that as men, it then becomes their duty to take responsibility, care for themselves, their families and communities. This is an achievable feat but only if the minds of these young boys are nurtured properly as children. I believe the totality of being a man starts in the womb of his mother and ends with the lessons he learns from life.

The lady or the tramp

We are losing our precious little girls to videos, "ballas and shot callas." Female children as young as five years old are dancing as seductive as strippers because of their exposure to certain music/dance videos, and home environments. Even the clothing of these children makes the little girls appear older, and what's worse, as parents we are spending lots of money buying the clothes! What happened to the frilly type clothing adorned in lace with the matching gloves and socks? Does that type of clothing still exist?

We must introduce our girls to life accompanied with love, structure, guidance, and discipline. Convey the significance of educating the mind, the importance of feminine hygiene, the dangers of sexual transmitted infections and the appropriate ways to dress and communicate. If we are trying to prepare our girls to become women, the lessons of life must begin immediately, not during puberty.

Little girls love attention; they love being told they are pretty and loved. If they are not hearing these words at home, they will often respond inappropriately when they hear these words from someone outside of the home. They will begin to associate compliments with love. This is why it is so important to talk with them about life.

They need to know they are capable of loving and complimenting themselves. They need to know just because a man tells them they are beautiful, isn't justification for intimacy.

Make them aware of their body parts and please use the correct names; little girls do not have a "pocket book" between their legs, they have a vagina. Warn them of the dangers of being touched inappropriately by others and make them feel comfortable enough to tell you if someone does touch them. Be cautious of the people who are in the presence of your girl and don't force her to sit on anyone's lap or kiss others on the cheek. Don't teach your babies to love everyone because everyone will not love them in return.

Most importantly, love your girls. Don't become jealous or compete with them as they become older. Instead, look at the accomplishment you've made by watching the growth of your young lady. She will never be able to outsmart you because you were the adult first, you will have everlasting wisdom that she will continue to benefit from throughout her life.

The goal is to make sure she grows to be an outstanding young lady, not a tramp. Her clothing should not make her appear older; she shouldn't be made the life of the party by performing the latest adult dances in front of adult guests.

If you want to highlight her talents, ask her to read a book in front of the guests or showcase her honor roll certificate, but depending on the time of the party, she should be in bed anyway. Stress the importance of education and responsibility versus name brand clothes and hairstyles.

It seems more times than not, whenever a mother has a child who is out of control, an irresponsible man is somewhere in the midst. During his presence, the single mother is totally consumed with trying to raise him instead of raising her children, this includes attempts to persuade him to secure gainful employment and treat her better.

If we (women) are responsible for birthing future generations, we have to make sure our minds are prepared for the challenges that come along with such a great responsibility. Raising children is a difficult task but the overall experiences of raising good children definitely outweigh all difficulties.
DO YOUR JOB AND DO IT WELL!

Education

I cannot stress the importance of being involved with our children's education! It is imperative to start at an early age. Learning does not start when children enter school; it begins while the baby is in the womb of its mother. The key to a child's academic success begins with teachings from the parents. **We are our children's first teacher.** Children learn their vocabulary skills from parents, they learn morals and values from parents, and children also learn racism and bigotry from parents.

Immediately upon enrolling children into school, parents should become familiar with the school's staff and administrators. Meetings with the teacher must be engaged often to discuss strategies to enhance academic success. Parents must not show up only when the child exhibits behavior problems, appropriate measures of discipline should take place at home so teachers will not be responsible for babysitting unruly children.

There are several reasons why some parents are not involved in their child's education. One of those reasons is intimidation; some parents feel intimidated by teachers and other school personnel. This intimidation prevents them from attending parent-teacher meetings and causes fear of talking with teachers about the child's academic status. Some parents feel their children will never be successful academically because the parents themselves weren't successful as students.

Studies have shown that children perform extremely well in the classroom when they receive academic reinforcement at home.

When children spend less time in front of the television and more time reading books, their chances of becoming high achievers will increase. Furthermore, a family's socio-economic status is not a predictor of academic success; parental support, determination, and dedication determine success.

It is clear that the public school system cannot be relied on to help our children reach academic achievement. The classrooms are overcrowded, the teachers are overwhelmed and underpaid, many of the schools are underfunded and do not have the necessary supplies/equipment to ensure high levels of academic achievement. Other issues that may weaken academic success include children going to school hungry, mentally diminished as the result of neglect, sexual and /or physical abuse. The most severe problem is the diagnosis of mental disorders in these students, especially Black male students.

Today, Black children are being diagnosed with mental disorders in astronomical proportions. The most common disorders include mental retardation, and attention-deficit/hyperactivity disorder (ADHD). As a result of the diagnosis, teachers spend more time modifying behavior than teaching.

After the diagnosis is made, these students are often prescribed psychotropic medication and/or immediately placed in special education classes. It is believed that once the student is placed in an environment among other students with special needs, the child will have an equal opportunity for educational growth. However, this type of placement often lowers the self-esteem of these children and there isn't much educational growth.

In fact, most of these students drop out of school and enter their adult life as illiterate and/or apart of the penal system.

Education Solutions

Some parents aren't able to afford the tuition of private education, so public schools are the only choice. There is still hope. Understand that your child's education is about **your child**, not about you; get over your fears and unfortunate experiences about school. Teach your child as much as you can at home; don't make the assumption that the school system will properly educate your child. Educating your child should be your primary goal.

Educate your children in the areas that aren't taught in the classroom. Teach them the history of Africa and its people. Tell them that Africa is a CONTINENT not a country. Teach them that someday they should visit a country in Africa to behold the beauty and breathe the air of the true homeland. Make them realize the history of African people **did not** begin during their enslavement. While it is true the enslavement of our ancestors was a hideous part of our history, it is not our entire history! Tell them the truth about who we were, what we did, who we are and what we are capable of continuing to do. However, in doing so, remember we are not capable of educating our children about our people if we don't know who we are as individuals.

Help your children with homework and converse often with their teachers and other school administrators (school principal, guidance counselors, etc.). Don't rely solely on your child to tell you how he/she is performing in school. Ask for progress reports and report cards. Become familiar with the school's calendar for important dates such as school holidays, teacher planning days, midterm/final exam days and dates of progress reports and report cards.

Make sure your child understands that he/she is 100% responsible for their academic success. They need to accept responsibility early in life for their actions/behaviors. This is important so the child will not become an adult who blames everyone else for his/her failures.

Go to school with your child at least three times per school year. I literally mean GO TO SCHOOL WITH YOUR CHILD. Attend each class, don't ask any questions of the teacher during class instruction, just sit and observe. Although you want your children to do their job in the classroom, you also want to make sure the teachers are doing their job. When the teacher knows that you are visiting, most will be on their best behavior, but remember the goal here is to OBSERVE. Observe the other students, if the teacher is teaching or acting differently, you will be able to detect this difference in the reaction of the students.

Demand the hiring of **QUALIFIED** teachers in your child's school. Just because your child attends a school located in a lower economic neighborhood is no excuse for the school board to approve the hiring of substandard teachers. If your child's teacher cannot speak proper grammar, proper grammar skills are not being taught in the classroom, if your child's teacher cannot write effectively, writing skills are not being taught in the classroom.

Teaching at minority schools should not be viewed as a last resort occupation. That should be a slap in the face to all qualified teachers! It seems when an individual can't find other employment, they teach.

I realize the current academic curriculum is somewhat different from the past curriculum of parents. Because of this, some parents are unable to help their children with homework. In such cases, tutors are essential. While every parent may not be able to afford the $20.00 an hour fee for a tutor, there are solutions. Visit the education department of the local universities and inquire about free tutors. Other ways include talking with the school's guidance counselor or other parents for tutoring information. Visit the local community centers and inquire about free tutoring services, call the local NAACP and ask for assistance with finding those who may be available to help your children. Attend the monthly school board meetings and let your voice be heard regarding the academic concerns of your child.

If none of these ideas prove to be successful, contact the superintendent of schools for additional assistance. Make your voice heard.

Correct your child's grammar. Don't believe the hype about "Ebonics." It's not our language and our people should not claim it in our community, and it definitely should not be an acceptable way of speaking by our children. Children should be told that speaking grammatically correct and achieving academic excellence doesn't mean "talking and acting White."

If using the correct grammar is talking White, what defines talking Black? If making good grades means being White, does being a failure define being Black?

Take frequent trips to the public library. Obtain a library card and encourage its use. This will often ensure a love of reading and thirst for knowledge. Take advantage of the free computer services at the local libraries. In order for our children to be competitive in the job market, it is mandatory they become computer literate. Being able to create a page on face book does not qualify as being computer literate and neither does being the neighborhood Madden football champion (Wii).

Challenge what they are being taught in school; force them to think critically about what they are being told by others. Explain that there is nothing wrong with asking questions and seeking truth. Knowing and speaking truth is the only way to truly be free; freedom of one's mind leads to freedom of the body, soul and spirit.

Just as we want our children to listen to us, we must listen to them. Stop believing everything the teacher tells you about your child. There should be nothing a complete stranger can tell you about your child that you don't already know. Yes, there will be times when your child will exhibit behavior in the classroom that you aren't aware of.

Yes, the day will come when your precious angels will use words that will totally knock you off your feet.

I remember when my daughter was a 2nd grade student. At the end of each school day, I would ask her about her day. On this particular afternoon, after asking my usual questions, she explained to me that she learned about "breath detects." After asking her to define that term, she looked at me and said, "Ma, you're a grown up, you don't know about breath detects?" Needless to say, I felt extremely shallow at that moment. However, I sucked up my embarrassment and told her no. She then explained that sometimes children are born with no arms and no legs. After laughing uncontrollably for about 15 minutes, I calmly told my darling daughter the correct pronunciation is birth defects. She looked at me with this strange look on her face and said, "That's what I said, breath detects." If I wasn't an alert parent, an attempt may have been made to convince me that my daughter was experiencing speech and language delays.

All children are full of surprises and all children like to see how much mischief they can get away with. However, parents should recognize severe problems such as behavior and emotional problems, bad study habits, reading and math deficiencies, immediately. How does a mother not realize that her ten-year-old child is illiterate?

There are so many homes with toys, electronic games, over priced shoes and clothes, but not many items to embrace learning. Where are the books, pens, pencils, paper, calculators and computers? Make the appropriate changes, strive to save the minds of your precious little ones, become dedicated to saving their lives! Take this opportunity to learn with your children.

Instill consequences for unwanted behavior. Don't send your child and his/her behavior problems to the schools for someone else to deal with. Deal with your own children and make them suffer consequences for unwanted behavior. Don't allow them to be labeled because your parenting skills are weak. Often, there is nothing wrong with these children other than being the product of bad parenting.

Children need to understand that education is essential to their survival. The most important lessons will take place outside of the classroom. Education is a life-long process; every situation in life is a lesson. What is most damaging to us as a people is what we have made a choice *not* to learn. For example, we make a conscience effort to enroll our boys in sporting activities as early as five years old.

If we as parents were to make mathematics, literacy and comprehension our primary focus, wouldn't our children be as dominant in the classroom as they are on the football fields and basketball courts? We have made a choice not to focus or value academics, and we are suffering miserably because of that choice.

Television

Turn it off!!

Dating

Some single mothers will devote most or all of their attention to the men in their lives. Some mothers will sacrifice their children's health, safety, and life just to maintain relationships with men. This mistake has caused many children their sanity and/or lives.

While writing the manuscript for this book, I was watching the Oprah Winfrey Show, and the guests were discussing the subject of child molestation. I was quite intrigued by the comments of one mother who explained to the audience that she knew her boyfriend was raping her son. She further explained how she would sleep on the floor at night in front of her bedroom door in an attempt to protect her son from further abuse. I was appalled! Instead of leaving and having the boyfriend arrested, she chose to stay with him!

She chose to continue the relationship with the rapist of her child, and believed by sleeping in front of their bedroom door at night, the abuse would stop. That is so insane! Who said rape only occurs at night? It occurs when the opportunity presents itself.

Taking the innocence of a child is the most horrid act imaginable, but when the mother knows this is happening and does nothing to protect the child, she too should be prosecuted. How can a mother sleep comfortably with the man who has raped her child?

Women, there is no excuse for this!! Believe your children when they tell you someone is hurting them. The word *mother* is so powerful in the mind of a child. They believe we have magic powers to fix anything. When they have a problem, the first person they want to comfort them is their mother.

The ability to give birth is a gift from God that should not be abused or neglected in any way. We are powerful beings and we have the ability to do something that no man can. We should cherish that gift every day and give praise to the most high for this wonderful blessing.

Although it is true that it takes a village to raise a child, the members of the village must be healthy both mentally and physically if the children in the village are expected to be healthy mentally and physically. Some of the people in the village are evil and should never have contact with our children. Some of these wicked people are neighbors, family members, close friends, community and church leaders, teachers, and some are even mothers, fathers, husbands and boyfriends. Wake up women, protect your children the way you would want someone to protect you. They cannot protect and care for themselves. We must carefully choose the village and villagers we want to help us raise our children.

Take your time when getting to know a man. Please don't force your children to call the new man in your life daddy after only two weeks of dating. You hardly know him, so what makes you think that after a couple of movies and dinner, he is *daddy*? Make every attempt to be his friend.

Talk about your future goals as well as his. Where does he want to go? How does he plan to get there? Does he have a spiritual foundation? Does he vote? How much does he know about politics, the criminal justice system? What type of relationship does he have with his mother, why isn't he married, what does he read, does he know how to read? Does he have children? If so, does he provide moral and financial support for those children? Does he even like children? These questions and many others are essential when getting to know a man. These questions will also scare him away if he really isn't interested in getting to know you. If he does decide to run, let him go.

Children watch everything we do. If we are in an abusive relationship, our children will be affected by that exposure and exhibit the damaging symptoms of that exposure. Many young girls, who witness their mother's abuse, often become adults who date abusive men. Young boys who witness this abuse are usually angry as children and become angrier adults. This anger is then taken out on their girlfriend or wife. This is how the cycles begins, but remember, whatever we start, we can end. Break the cycle.

Your love can't save him

O.k., so we've all been blinded by what we thought was love at some point in our lives. As women we can all remember that one guy we were sure was THE ONE!!

We also knew he was sleeping with other women, we knew he only came around when we had money, we knew he was a liar and the truth wasn't in him! Yes, we knew all of this! Yet, we stayed and loved him even more. Why, because we were sure, our love could save him.

Now, I am not talking about our first school-girl crush or a high school sweetheart. I am referring to those unfortunate learning experiences we've had as grown women. I can remember as if it were yesterday……..

I was standing in the financial aid line at Florida Agricultural and Mechanical University (FAMU), I saw this smooth, chocolate brother staring at me. Although he was receiving love from everybody in the room, he was still looking at me the entire time. I glanced at him for a second but my mind was on my check (yes, it was late).

As I left the office I heard, "Excuse me?" I turned around and it was him, smooth chocolate. I played it cool and answered kindly by saying, "Yes, may I help you?" He asked if I was from Miami, FL because of the Miami tee shirt I was wearing, and that's how it began. He turned out to be a really nice person. I later learned he was also a student at FAMU and he was a football player. We became friends and then lovers, and he was a great lover! I mean he could put a chill in my bones on a day when it was 90 degrees outside! I thought I had myself something! Well, I did---I had a guy who had a different woman for every night of the week. I knew he was no-good because people told me, and I saw him with different women.

Nevertheless, his lies were as sweet and sensual as his loving. However, I had a plan. I was going to love and continue to be there to show him that I was the true woman for him. I just knew my love would turn him around and change his mind. Child please, I was so crazy. That man kept me and all the other women around as long as we decided to put up with him and each other. The lesson learned, if he doesn't want you, leave him alone-*Your love can't save him.*

The Truth

Being a single mother isn't a handicap. It does not mean your life has come to an end, nor does it mean you are a failure. It does mean however, you have many challenges ahead of you. Take this opportunity to get to know yourself and your children. Before you decide to invite a man into your lives (you and the children), discover the things you will accept, will not accept and which things you are willing to compromise.

There will be several temporary struggles to endure, but remember those struggles are just that---temporary. Don't show your contempt for men in front of your children. Don't be upset with *all* men because of the pain caused by *one* man. Regardless of what you heard, all men are not the same. All Black men are not dogs! All Black men do not abandon their children! So what if you've been hurt, have you fully analyzed the situation to determine how you played a part in the destruction of the relationship? It's not his fault every time. No one comes to the table with clean hands, sometimes the dirt of a woman is just concealed a little better.

You have to evaluate and choose a man the same way you would a pint of strawberries. Let me explain this concept. By the time the strawberries arrive at the market, someone else has already planted the seed and provided everything else to ensure healthy growth. By the time you arrive at the market, there are ripe strawberries everywhere, waiting for *you to choose them*. When shopping for strawberries, you peruse your choices to make sure all of the strawberries are perfect or close to it. Because they are wrapped in plastic, you are unable to physically pick through or taste them before deciding to take them home; you have to decide based on the outer appearance. However, no matter how perfect the majority of the strawberries look, there is always one or two in the package that are damaged. This is discovered once the wrapping is removed.

Once the damaged strawberries are identified, they are quickly discarded. If you're paying attention, you notice that the *majority* of the strawberries are good. In that majority, some are big, some are sweet, some are hard and some are soft, but you still know to quickly discard the damaged ones. There will even be those that look a little peculiar, but if you feel they have potential, they will be washed and kept, nevertheless. These precautions are taken because you know at some point these strawberries will enter your body, and your choice to keep only the good ones will hopefully satisfy your hunger and desire for the taste of a good strawberry. You know if you choose to digest the unhealthy ones, you may become ill and suffer negative consequences because of that choice.

You see ladies, the mothers of these men have given birth and raised them, and whether she raised them properly or not, the bottom line is they (the men) don't need another mother. After you choose your man, the majority of your time together should not be spent trying to raise him. Just like the strawberry, the man was already grown when you met him. When you chose your strawberry, your intention was not to re-plant it in an effort to re-grow it. Your assumption when you purchased it, was that it possessed everything needed to satisfy you.

There are both good and bad men in the world, you have to choose wisely. The external appearance of a man is seen first, once you take the time to get to know him, that external layer is slowly removed to reveal his internal character. Once it is revealed, who do you see? Is he one that should be kept or quickly discarded?

There are many women who are involved in relationships with good men. Even in these situations, we still manage to mess up. We talk too damn much about nothing, we listen to jealous friends who don't have anyone or anything in their lives, and we play immature games that cause those good men not to trust us any longer. So many good men are trapped in relationships with foolish women because these women cannot let go. These women either threaten to take everything he has or refuse to allow him to see his children if he attempts to leave. Let it go, let him go, you had your chance with him, now it's over.

Some single mothers feel they can make it without a man because a single mother raised them without a man. Well, the truth is, there are several things you can do without a man, but there is so much more you can do with a man. Please stop lying to your selves by saying, "I don't need a man." The Creator did not put us on this earth to be alone. We may not need a man to pay our bills or to make us feel good about ourselves; however, there is a certain completion that can only be achieved by the healthy, supportive union of a woman **and** a man.

How do we expect our sons to bring home beautiful, intelligent Black women if our sons watch us mistreat other Black men?

Our sons will not only despise us, but every woman who looks like us. How will our daughters know what healthy love between a Black male and female is, if they continue to hear nothing but stereotypical descriptions of Black men? Because of our own insecurities, we are creating chaos in the minds of our children.

Chapter 3

Educated Women

"Facing this undesirable result, the highly educated Negro often grows sour. He becomes too pessimistic to be a constructive force and usually develops into a chronic fault-finder or a complainant at the bar of public opinion."

-Carter G. Woodson

There was a time when a member of the family would leave home to attend college and return a pillar of the community. Today's college student has become so *educated* that the family hates when she comes home to visit. The student returns home with disgust for everything! She no longer talks with childhood friends, the family house is no longer comfortable because the furniture is too run down, and the grammar of the other family members becomes an embarrassment. Today's college graduate must understand that a college education is not an individual feat but a triumph for the entire family and community. We cannot forget the many sacrifices that others have made and the road our ancestors paved for us all to be able to obtain a college education.

A woman should strive to be educated in all spheres of life, along with having a thorough understanding that education is not limited to the classroom.

Education should provide the knowledge necessary to continue personal growth, and the uplift of others. That knowledge shouldn't be used to make a mockery of others who are less fortunate nor should it be used to intimidate those in the community. Knowledge is the mother of wisdom; we have to know something before we are able to share anything with others.

The mind cannot be replaced or reproduced, handle it with care

During our ancestors' enslavement, they were whipped, tortured and/or lynched for many reasons. One of those reasons included knowing how to read. If someone is willing to end the life of another because of his or her ability to read, that should be an indicator of how powerful reading is! As women, we should make reading a part of our every day ritual. Read everything! Read material that you agree with, as well as material you disagree with, learn more today than you knew yesterday.

There are many issues being discussed and debated relating to women, and we should be familiar with most, if not all of those issues. We should also be powerful participants during any forums and law making decisions regarding us. Reading various materials to broaden our mind will allow us that opportunity. Our education should be used as a tool of empowerment; empowering the people to rise above their circumstances with the challenge of taking someone with them.

College degree or wife to be

I received my degrees from FAMU and I loved every minute of the FAMU experience! Deciding to attend college was one of the best decisions I've ever made. I learned so much about the value of a college education, the culture of other students, the importance of giving back to the community, the joy of reading and the mentality of *educated women*. Every woman comes to college with a different goal. Some want to become teachers and help change the world, others have dreams of becoming lawyers, engineers, or doctors, and some women just want to find a man.

Some actually attempt to select their husbands based on the type of degree he is receiving. According to the *educated woman,* the best husbands are found in the school of Business and Industry (SBI), college of pharmacy, pre- med, or pre-law. The assumption is these graduates will at some point provide a comfortable lifestyle.

Of course, these students aren't being schooled about being a husband or the ways to treat a woman.

So knowing this, why do we look for men with the most money making potential to be our husbands, and why do Black women continue to become upset when Black men refer to them as gold diggers? If money were the only thing it took to make a happy home, Juanita would still be married to Michael Jordan.

If money is so important to you, make and save your own money. Don't stroll the college yard looking into the eyes of young men to determine how much money they will be worth in 10 years. How much money will you be worth?

Suppose men decided to stroll the yard looking for women who are enrolled in the schools of pharmacy or business; with great credit; wearing her *real* hair and nails and not sexually active. How many of us would still be single?

What if, in a perfect world, women enrolled in college with the primary goal of improving the community? What if we were taught as young children how important we are to those communities? What if as women, we began to educate ourselves about our history, because of the dire need to heal the pain that so many of us continue to feel? What if we believed that we are capable of saving ourselves because the Creator loved us so much that He provided us with everything we needed to survive? If only we lived in a perfect world.

High yellow, red bone and sexy chocolate

These names, along with variations of skin color often cause friction between Black females (children and adults). Some of the lighter skinned women feel they are entitled to certain privileges because their skin is closer to white, while darker skinned women are often viewed as angry, ignorant and less attractive because their skin is darker.

This thought process is not limited to adults; I have heard children (boys and girls) as young as ten years old make statements about not wanting to play outside during the summer months because they fear "turning black." The sickness doesn't stop there. Some women prefer to only date and have sex with men who have lighter skin because they believe there's a greater chance of giving birth to a pretty baby.

Variations of our skin tones should never dictate beauty or intelligence. Nor should it define who is Black or who isn't Black enough.

There are some women who feel so insecure about themselves due to years of being mocked, bullied and abused as children, because of their dark skin. Some of them have been mentally beat down so much, they can't see how naturally beautiful they are.

You need to perm yo nappy hair

Recently a white male television personality made a disrespectful comment about a group of female college basketball players. He called the Black team members "nappy-headed hoes." Ultimately, he was fired because of that comment as well as past racial comments. The argument was then made that hard-core rap artists should also stop using words that degrade Black women. This argument can be made all day but until we, as a Black community start respecting and treating ourselves better, the world will continue to call us nappy-headed hoes and other words that we use so freely.

During the 1960's, wearing "natural" hairstyles was the norm. Both men and women proudly wore their beautiful, tightly curled hair either braided or in an Afro style. They truly believed black was beautiful and felt no need to alter their blackness. Hair has always been a sign of strength as early as the biblical days of Sampson.

Today unfortunately, Black women who choose to wear the natural styles are often accused of being militant, Afro-centric, "conscience" or wearing their blackness on their sleeves. I am one of those women who proudly wear my hair in its natural texture and I LOVE IT!!

One of the many dilemmas with women who have chemically treated hair is **some** of them are accused of trying to be white and unfortunately, this is true. Other women just the like the various styles of permed hair as well as the softer texture, and have no thoughts of being or acting like anyone except a Black woman.

While, there is nothing wrong with wearing our hair any way we choose, I am concerned that some of us believe beauty is defined as having long, straight, bouncy hair. Where did we learn this lesson? Was that the message of our mothers when they started processing our hair when we were children? Was it Madame CJ Walker's invention of the hot comb? On the other hand, could it be that some women have fooled themselves into thinking that everyone else is beautiful except the natural Black woman?

There are times when no one is harder on us than we are. On any given day, you can hear children taunting one another by calling each other hurtful names because of the tone of their skin or the texture of their hair. We have been taught that our natural selves are ugly, shameful, and in much need of change. What other ethnic groups participate in this type of madness?

If a Black woman wakes up and decide to wrap her hair instead of combing it, that's alright. If she decides she doesn't want to wear any make up to enhance her looks, that's fine too. If she decides to wear a pair of sweat pants and a tee-shirt to the store, instead of name brand jeans, that's her choice and she should not be ridiculed. We have everything we need to be beautiful.

Black women and girls around the globe----WE ARE BEAUTIFUL JUST THE WAY WE ARE!! Carry this message in your heart, in your soul, in your stride when you walk, in the words you speak when you talk---take it with you and let it consume you. Let me assure you, we are just fine.

Historically Black Colleges and Universities

There are over 100 HBCUs* throughout the United States of America and as stated earlier, I am the alumna of one of the greatest----FAMU (est. 1887 Tallahassee, FL). You would think all Black people would be proud of the long-standing tradition of HBCU graduates, especially when there were so many other universities with policies

---

* See Appendix B

preventing the enrollment of Black students. Never the less, the devastating effect of the enslaved mind has caused many Blacks to turn their backs on HBCUs. Many feel HBCU graduates do not receive a credible education; if it ain't white, it ain't right.

After I made the decision to attend FAMU, I was told by some that I was limiting myself by attending an HBCU because the world was not all black. I thought about that for a moment. After the moment had passed, I began remembering my primary school experience as a student enrolled in white schools. There was no concern or conversation about the world being all white. As a matter of fact, the lower the Black student enrollment, the happier the school staff seemed to be. Other than a small section in the history books about Martin Luther King, Jr., there was no mention of blackness, culture, or the many facts that Blacks played such important roles in the nation building of America. With that said, I wonder how many Black people are informing white schools that they are limiting their students by not incorporating African-American History.

The goals of HBCUs do not include teaching racism. These graduates do not walk across the stage during commencement with thoughts of causing harm to the nearest White person. There is nothing wrong with having such an insatiable hunger to want more, and if that hunger is satisfied by obtaining an education for us, by us, then so be it. I applaud every student who has the courage to endure the criticisms, the wrinkled faces of others and any other negative feedback because of the students' choice to attend an HBCU. These graduates embark on every professional career that exists.

The real task however, begins after the commencement ceremony is over. What are we doing with the education, skills and knowledge we received? How are we utilizing that education to help others? Have we realized the skills we obtained make us servants of our communities? Do we understand the importance of sharing that knowledge with those who are depending on us to return and give them hope for a better tomorrow? It is important that we receive college degrees, but it's more important to give back to our communities.

Giving back can be more than the summer football camps for the neighborhood children. It does not benefit a Black male to become a pro athlete and remain illiterate. Summer reading, math, and science camps, are **ALWAYS** beneficial. The students often forget these subject matters during summer vacation, but repetition will ensure adequate comprehension of each subject.

Accountants can be instrumental in developing early-learning math programs in the daycare centers and the adults can be educated about the advantages of investing their monies and starting retirement plans. Athletes (pro and non-pro) are always welcome to return to the local recreation centers and start exercise programs. Currently, there are too many obese children who are suffering from diabetes and other diseases as a result of being overweight.

Educators possess the knowledge and skills to develop yearly reading programs in each of the lower socio-economic neighborhoods. Competitiveness is also determined by the level of reading skill and word knowledge. As stated in chapter 2, we will not accept *Ebonics* as an acceptable language for our children.

Published authors can visit the local schools to encourage students to write their own stories. Go back and read to the children, start a junior book club for children, and if possible, invest in having the books (written by the students) published.

Doctors and nurses can provide outreach programs to educate about healthy eating habits, exercise programs, the dangers of obesity, hypertension, diabetes, cardiac disease and certain cancers.

Lawyers can initiate bi-monthly criminal justice workshops to educate both adults and neighborhood youth about the various laws and any new statutes. Law enforcement officers can collaborate with those lawyers to discuss the importance of neighborhood safety and community policing, as well as addressing any citizen concerns. The officers can also discuss appropriate vs. inappropriate behavior of those approached by a law enforcement officer; these discussions can possibly decrease police brutality and the number of *justifiable* homicides.

Some entertainers have the financial fortitude to improve school structures, or at the very least furnish existing schools with new books, computers, and other school supplies. This would definitely benefit the children of that community more than having a car show, which many times cause children to view material objects as more important than an education.

Politicians should make sure the laws being discussed, debated, and passed are relevant to the survival of the people as a whole. They should discontinue the practice of showing up in minority neighborhoods and church events only during elections. It is great that the black vote is so important, but so are the people and their needs. Politicians should make it a practice of being accessible at all times, not just during elections.

Social workers are unfairly known as those who remove children from their homes, and many times, they do, but that is just one part of their job. In an effort to remove the "bad guy" label, social workers can establish parenting classes in the neighborhood centers. During those classes, dialogue regarding acceptable vs. unacceptable behavior in the presence of a child should take place. Parents and children will know the facts/myths of corporal punishment and abuse. This type of dialogue can also help parents, and children understand the laws and state statues regarding families and children.

Let us not only give back to our communities but to our Alma Maters. If we are afraid that our donations will be mismanaged, ask questions and demand answers. We can no longer complain about the outdated buildings of our universities if we are unwilling to help finance new construction.

The key is to become involved with everything! Make decisions, make sacrifices and make as much noise as possible to make sure HBCUs continue to graduate intelligent, caring and giving individuals. We cannot risk our schools being closed because of financial neglect or being merged with other universities that do not have our best interest at the forefront of their curriculum, goals, or mission.

As HBCU graduates, we should not only want to be involved, we should demand change about anything that makes us look less than who we are—a proud people who have yet to be beaten or destroyed by ANYTHING!

We have always been an intelligent people and we should be determined to carry on a legacy of intelligence, perseverance, and strength.

Chapter 4

Married Women

"It is beneficial to your marriage to truly understand who he is and respect the very essence of his being."

-Author

So, he asked you to marry him and you said yes. The happy family begins; mother, father and child, there should be no dilemmas. Wrong! Even after a woman becomes a wife, she continues to be desperate.

You have him, but are you prepared to do the things to keep him? What is your role in the marriage? What is his role? What are the roles of both of you regarding your children? Does he work while you're caring for the children and the home? Are you working while he is caring for the children and the home? Are you both working? Why? Why not?

Many women are under the impression that marriage will automatically create fireworks, the lovemaking will become so intense stars are seen for two days. Some believe there will be no arguing, the house will be filled with love and joy, and the children will always make the right choices because they are being raised in a two parent, stable home.

This is such a wonderful scenario but it is not a reality. The reality is, marriage is hard work. It takes ***prayer, love, communication, patience, forgiveness, understanding, support, sharing, caring and compromise.***

Another startling reality is we are losing our men to other women because in many cases, we don't know how to treat them nor do we know how to love them. We don't establish the appropriate roles before we say 'I do' and are often times disappointed with the outcome. Just when we thought we knew everything about him, we will discover a couple of new things. As soon as a small storm surfaces, we are ready to pack up and leave.

How have you defined your perfect man? Did you determine his worth based on his income or the type of car he drives? If so, not only have you defined his worth but you have also defined yourself as a gold digger. There is nothing wrong with expecting a man to provide for his family, but money doesn't determine how much he loves you or that he loves you at all, nor does it mean he knows how to treat you.

The heart of a real woman is never satisfied with money alone. She is capable of looking beyond material possessions; she is able to recognize the bigger picture. A man's spirituality, heart, actions and conversation determine his worth. If he loves you, he will take care of you, and his family will always be his first priority. You should never attempt to force a man to love you; he either loves you or he doesn't.

Establishing a relationship with his family and friends will not bring him closer to you, and spending your hard-earned money buying gifts for him definitely will not make him love you.

I believe women are the smartest creatures to grace this earth and although we ignore so many of the signs, we know the truth about ourselves and the men in our lives. In knowing these truths, we must admit we have work to do; we have to step up to the plate if our families and men are to be saved. To stand before the Creator, family and friends and profess your love for each other is the most significant thing a couple can do. It is right in the eyes of God and it is the most appropriate thing to do before deciding to have children.

It is beneficial to your marriage to understand who your husband is and respect the very essence of his being. Understand that although he lives in a nation built by his own, he also lives in a society created to destroy him. Because of his will to survive, he leaves his family everyday to face the world and demand that part which belongs to him. Yet, these men endure because deep down inside, although no one else identifies them as such, they know they are men; men who are willing to care for and feed their families by any means necessary. As a wife, how can you support this man and all of his efforts?

Love yourself

You support your husband by being confident in who you are. Don't change who you are just to make him love you. Remember, he saw something special in you before you became his wife. You can't possibly support someone mentally or physically if you are not equipped to face yourself each day.

Loving yourself includes making sure your mental and physical health is intact. If you are experiencing some difficulties that require the assistance of a mental health professional, don't be ashamed to seek those services. Make frequent visits to your primary care physician, eat healthier, and exercise regularly to prevent the health problems that are so prevalent in our community such as hypertension, diabetes, high cholesterol, cardiac disease, and obesity. There is always room for growth within everyone, recognize the areas you need to improve, make the necessary adjustments and love yourself first!

Choose him over everything else

Pray for your husband, pray with your husband. Create a home for him, a sacred place where he feels safe and secure. When he comes home to you at the end of the day, let him know that he, your king, is in his kingdom. If he has to deal with so much chaos outside of his home, the last thing he needs is to come home to a less than peaceful environment. Don't be afraid to follow your husband (if he's mentally stable). Let him know that you trust him and knows that he will not lead you in harm's way. Show interest in his day, show that you are concerned about him and not just concerned if he made enough money to pay the mortgage.

Keep your home dirt free

Cleanse your home of evil spirits and terrible people that may attempt to destroy your family.
If you have people in your life who aren't in the corner of you and your family, they should be removed immediately. If you do not remove them, your attention will quickly be diverted from your husband and his attention will be diverted from you and onto someone else.

Cleanse your home of dirty dishes and soiled clothing. I am amazed at the number of women who appear in public neatly dressed and meticulously manicured but do not take pride in keeping a clean home. My grandmother often told me that a woman who doesn't keep her house clean, is a woman who doesn't keep her body clean.

Love your husband for who he is and accept what he has to offer you. Don't compare him to your friends' husbands and don't compare him to your ex-lovers. If you married him and agreed to love and honor the man that he is, you have to accept who he is. Comparing him to other men is a sure recipe for disaster. If he does not quite measure up to someone from your past, for whatever reason (finance, sex, physical appearance, etc), you will soon resent him and regret marrying him. While that is unfair to him, the amount of stress that will occur as a result is also unfair to you. You may soon discover that the 'worse' in your marriage will develop much quicker than the 'better.'

Other than being a great man, your husband is human. The day will arrive when your husband looks or comment about the physique of another woman. This is no reason for you to become enraged or think you are less attractive in his eyes. Remember, you are the one he married, this is not the time to show your insecurities, work them out before you become someone's wife.

Don't tell your friends all of your business, especially your bedroom business. A woman should always have a smile on her face that others wonder about. If that smile is because of the love your husband made to you the night before or the rose he placed on your pillow early that morning, that smile should remain between you and your husband, not between you and your girls.

Don't brag or boast to other women about what your husband does or his ability to provide for you. Boasting has always led to catastrophic results. Not long ago, I was present at a luncheon with a group of women. One woman (we'll call her Debra), was married to a financially stable man and she wanted everyone to know it. She often talked about the things he purchased for her including the new car she received on Valentine's Day and the rather large house he built for the family. She also mentioned how excited she was about the fact he paid cash for her new vehicle and she didn't have to worry about a monthly car payment. Well, what she didn't realize (at that time) was one of the other women at the same luncheon also received a new car, paid for by Debra's husband.

You see, Debra didn't understand that as the wife, other women will always know who she is, but the wife will rarely know who the other woman is. Sometimes, as women we just need to be thankful for the blessings in our lives keep our mouths shut.

Make sure your female friends understand that your husband comes first. When your husband arrives home, he doesn't need to see the faces of your friends as soon as he walks through the door. He needs to see you, his wife with a big smile that's caused by his presence.

Listen to your husband

Listen to the things he says as well as the things he doesn't say. There will be times when he's not able to converse with you verbally. It is during those times, you have to utilize your female intuition. Listen to his heart, look into his eyes, read the lines in the palm of his hands. Know when he is hurting, know when he needs you, and prepare to deliver. Know when he is tired and what he needs to help him rest. He needs you to help him survive in this world.

Don't misunderstand his physical strength. Don't think just because he is strong physically he is capable of carrying the weight of the world on his shoulders indefinitely; everyone has a breaking point. Everyone needs help, including your husband. The question remains, now that you have him, are you prepared to do the things to keep him?

Can you stand the rain?

The number one reason for divorce in the United States is finance. It will cause some people to stay awake at night, lose their appetite, have a bad attitude, and in many cases, commit crimes. What would you do if your husband lost his job? How would you handle the situation if your husband gambled away the family savings? What if you discovered your husband was addicted to drugs/alcohol? Would you leave him? Would the vows you took no longer mean anything?

What if he decided that he wanted to pursue a college degree and asked you to become solely responsible for the bills, at least until he completed his degree? Would you agree to that? What if your husband was sentenced to serve time in prison? Would you divorce him? Would you be able to turn your love off as quickly as it was turned on? What if he had an affair? While these examples are mere scenarios to some, to others they are a reality. As a wife you have to be ready to act.

When you stated your vows, were there any stipulations? When you agreed to stay for better or worse, how did you define *worse*? Did worse mean infidelity? Did worse mean mental/physical abuse? Did worse mean finding out your husband is bi-sexual? What is your *worse*? As women we are so much alike, but with those similarities are many differences. One woman may be able to work it out with the husband who lost his job, another may have the strength to remain married to her husband after finding out he had an affair. Now, you have to decide what you can and cannot deal with.

Don't compare your strengths and weaknesses to those of another woman. Some women are true warriors who can handle just about anything thrown their way. Other women have yet to discover just how strong they are, and that's ok. This process is also a part of marriage, discovering the good and bad, strong and weak not only in our mate but in ourselves.

Marriage can be such a beautiful union. However, it takes work, lots of hard work from both the husband and wife.

Never challenge his manhood

HE is MAN, YOU are WOMAN! Never challenge the manhood of your husband. He realizes who he is, at times we don't realize who we are. That is understandable being that we are forced to wear so many hats in life. However, the one thing we are not is MAN, let your husband be who he is. Don't tear him down by calling him names that challenge his manhood. Don't embarrass your husband in public places, and NEVER curse him in front of the children. If this level of disrespect is shown toward him, your children will also begin to disrespect him.

Don't make the mistake of thinking that you are the head of the household because you have a higher annual income. He is the head of everything because God put him in that position. His finances do not make him the head, God made it so, and the quicker you realize that, the sooner you and your relationship will start to heal. Help him to live in peace and assist him with the day-to-day mental support that only his wife can provide.

Don't put undue pressure on him to provide you with things or a life style that he cannot afford. If your friend's house is larger, if she has a newer model car, if your friends are able to take a vacation out of the country each year, wish them well, be proud of them and ask them to send you a post card. Regarding your personal situation, please, love your husband for who he is and accept what he has to offer you. If you want that vacation to South Africa, make plans, make more money, get your finances in order and go!

There are so many subliminal messages attempting to let him know that he is less than a man. The most important person in his life (his wife) should be the one person to not only embrace his manhood, but also celebrate it.

The way to a man's heart is NOT through his stomach

I do not believe the way to a man's heart is through his stomach; I believe this is achieved by showing unwavering support at all times. A wife should be a husband's dream come true instead of his nightmare. Support his aspirations; when he talks about a lifelong dream of doing anything, support and encourage him! If you want to feed him, nourish his mind. Help him to discover the places inside of him that he didn't know existed. Help him uncover hidden talents that were buried so deep inside that after being discovered, he will forever be grateful to you.

Chapter 5

Remembering our Elders

The earliest memory of my legacy began with the birth of Mary E. Gennie. Mrs. Gennie was my grandmother and the light of my life. I'll always remember crying at the end of each summer vacation because I did not want to leave her. I can still smell the delicious aroma of macaroni and cheese, ho cakes, collard greens and fried chicken floating from her kitchen. I can also remember the winter vacations when the kerosene heater sitting in the middle of the floor warmed all of us.

Just the idea of going to spend time with my grandma, made my heart beat a little faster. Grandma was my everything, I loved her with every inch of my soul and I miss her dearly. Some of her favorite television shows were The Price is Right, As the World Turns, Good Times, and Sanford and Son. Watching TV during those times was a true family affair; the children sat and laughed, didn't talk during the program, there was no disrespect shown toward each other or toward the adults. Everyone knew grandma didn't play!

Grandma was never too busy to be grandma; she prayed, worked, cooked, cleaned, shopped, loved and cared for her family and everyone else in the neighborhood.

Today's youth have no idea about the joy of having a GRANDMA. I don't mean a grandmother, I'm talking about the elderly woman with graying hair, curved knuckles, slow gait, good cooking, sweet kisses and much advice and wisdom to share. I'm talking about the grandma who sits on the porch drinking ice water from an old jelly jar, the lady we looked forward to talking with when our mother wouldn't listen or just didn't seem to understand; the grandmas who asked you to scratch and grease her scalp on a hot summer's day.

Presently, some grandmothers are occupied with their own lives and too busy to talk with their grandchildren about anything. This can be attributed to the fact that mothers are giving birth much younger, which means the grandmothers are also much younger. Without the wisdom of our elders we will continue to suffer the ills of this world and perish because we have no idea where we are going. We have become disconnected from our elders, they are no longer sought for advice and they are no longer respected nor feared.

In the past, they were such important members of the family dynamic. The female elder was a valued source of strength for every family, neighborhood, and church. She represented so much more than age, she represented wisdom, knowledge, power, and everything else a woman should be, she was a survivor. The female elders of our past allowed the men to be men and made no attempts to take that role away from them.

They were also truly committed to their husbands and understood the importance of a stable family. This does not mean there were no problems in the home, but the way those problems were dealt with is the difference between now and then. For example, marriages remained intact even though husbands spent more time at the gambling hole than at home. Some even remained married after realizing their husbands had a second family, wives stayed close to their husbands even during difficult financial uncertainties.

Through all of this, the family remained together, their bond was unbreakable and we are here as a result. She endured the let downs and hurt that came along with her marriage quietly. She did not put her business in the street and she never talked against her husband in public. In other words, she did not help society define Black men negatively. She dealt with her house issues at home and left them there.

Her authority was never questioned and she was able to provide anything that was needed. Whether she was called madea, big momma, grandma, granny, or just 'ma; the bottom line is this---she was there and she did her job.

For me, the elders provided an opportunity to know what struggling to live was really about. They paid attention to everything, all of it was a lesson, and those lessons allowed them to survive to witness several generations. Some of those surviving elders are now residing in adult living facilities or nursing homes. Family members rarely return to visit and as a result, the mental and physical abuse of the elderly often goes unnoticed.

We must remember our elders; we must reach out to them and let them know how much we appreciate their sacrifices. Let them know that we would not be here had it not been for their blood, sweat and tears. Now is the time to say thank you and care for them the way they cared for us. We should feel so blessed because we're able to stand on the strength of their shoulders.

Although, we will never really know the totality of their struggles, I feel confident enough to state that we have endured no struggle that compare to theirs. They deserve our thanks and so much more.

Wisdom comes from our elders. Just to listen to them talk about their past lives is amazing. They should never be forgotten, we should always stand at attention in their presence because they have earned it.

To the elders of the past and present, please allow me this opportunity to say thank you. Thank you for living, thank you for the blood you shed, thank you for enduring and surviving the whips, chains, struggles, and many other injustices along your journey. Most of all, thank you for giving me the chance to live.

Epilogue

I am about Life

Through the body of a woman new life begins, we are everything to the world. We should demand respect at all times and command nothing less. We have the power to create love and war in the blink of an eye; that is power. No other being except woman can possess such power.

I am about life. Life begins and ends with women, but we must survive the struggles of life. There will be times when you feel like giving up. There will be times when you feel so insecure, and not like the person you see in the mirror. There will be times when you feel as if you're in this world all alone. You will experience days when others will make every attempt to beat you down mentally and physically. However, there will also be days when you feel as if you're on top of the world. The day will arrive when you will realize that you cannot be defeated. During that moment, you will confidently strut with your beauty in tow and others will say, "Who is that?" Well, your buoyancy will answer, "She is power, she is woman, she is you, and she is me."

This book was written in an attempt to save our families. I believe that women possess the capability to repair the breakdown of our family structure. If we become better women, mothers, sisters, and friends our men will follow.

We should not expect a knight in shining armor to sweep us off our feet if we are not prepared to be strong, sophisticated, intelligent queens to complete the circle of love. I know every woman will not benefit from reading this book, and this book wasn't written in an attempt to describe all Black women throughout the world. However, because there is at least one woman somewhere, who needs to know that someone else feels her pain, I could no longer keep silent. If you are that woman, this book is for you and you are not alone.

This book was also written as a result of my own desperation to feel wanted, appreciated and loved. That desperation would have destroyed me mentally had it not been for an awesome spiritual awakening. An awakening that boomed so loudly in my soul, telling me to love thyself! My soul was thirsting for truth and redemption. For so many years, my mind was shrinking from starvation, not realizing the power or the reality of enlightenment. My vision slowly started to blur because I had walked in darkness for so long. However, today is a new day, and I am desperate no more.

I now know that I am wanted, I am appreciated, and I am loved. I am ok, and to my beautiful sisters everywhere, so are you.

I know there are women who feel they did everything right; they were great mothers, wonderful friends, supportive wives, etc. Nevertheless, a child may still have gone astray, you may have felt the betrayal of a friend or spouse, or you may feel as if the Creator Himself has turned His back on you. To those women, I say this, do not give up, do not lose focus and don't forget who you are. Doing everything right doesn't mean everything will go our way.

We will continue to experience pain, disappointment, and loneliness. However, if at the end of the day you can look in the mirror and are pleased with who you are, and satisfied with your efforts, let go and let God.

Appendix –A

1. Anderson, Martin Lee (Panama City, FL 2006)
   *Died at age 14 while incarcerated at a youth detention facility in Bay County.

2. Bain, James (Lake Wales, FL 1974)
   *Served 35 years in prison for a crime he did not commit.

3. Bell, Sean (New York City, NY 2006)
   *Died at age 23, after police officers shot at his vehicle 50 times.

4. Brown, Barney (Hollywood, FL 1970)
   *At age 13, he was falsely accused of rape and spent 38 years in prison.

5. Crotzer, Alan (Tampa, FL 1981)
   *Incarcerated for 24.5 years for a crime he did not commit.

6. Diallo, Amadou (New York City, NY 1999)
   *Shot and killed at age 23 by 4 police officers. They fired a total of 41 shots.

7. Dorismond, Patrick (Brooklyn, NY 2000)
   *Shot and killed at age 26 by an undercover police officer.

8. Evans, Randolph (Brooklyn, NY 1976)
   *Shot in the head and killed at age 15 by a police officer claiming to be insane at the time of the shooting.

9. Graham, AJ (Tallahassee, FL 2009)
   *Falsely accused of armed robbery. Unable to attend his high school graduation due to his incarceration. The charges were eventually dropped.

10. Jena 6 (Jena, LA 2006)
    *Six teens charged with attempted murder after the beating of another student. After protests from outraged citizens, the charges were reduced.

11. Moore, Michael (Tallahassee, FL 2001)
    *Convicted at age 23 of rape, and sentenced to 30 years in prison.

12. Quincy Five (Quincy, FL 1971)
    *Five men convicted of the murder of a Leon county deputy sheriff. Although they were later exonerated, they were brutally beaten by law enforcement officers during their incarceration.

13. Victims of the FL Industrial School for Boys (Marianna, FL)
    *"The White House Boys" are the countless numbers of young boys who were raped, beaten, tortured, and murdered (including the bodies of those who were never found) while detained at the above juvenile detention facility.

14. Wilson, Genarlow (Douglasville, GA 2003)
    *At age 17, he was charged with aggravated child molestation and sentenced to 10 years in prison. This charge was the result of engaging in oral sex with a 15 year old classmate.

AND MANY MORE

Appendix-B

Historically Black Colleges and Universities

1. Alabama A&M University
2. Alabama State University
3. Albany State University
4. Alcorn State University
5. Allen University
6. Arkansas Baptist College
7. Barber-Scotia College Δ
8. Benedict College
9. Bennett College
10. Bethune-Cookman University
11. Bishop State Community College
12. Bluefield State College
13. Bowie State University
14. Central State University
15. Charles R. Drew University of Medicine and Science
16. Cheyney University of Pennsylvania
17. Claflin University
18. Clark Atlanta University
19. Clinton Junior College
20. Coahoma Community College
21. Concordia College
22. Coppin State University
23. Delaware State University
24. Denmark Technical College
25. Dillard University
26. Edward Waters College
27. Elizabeth City State University
28. Fayetteville State University
29. Fisk University
30. **FLORIDA A&M UNIVERSITY**

31. Florida Memorial University
32. Fort Valley State University
33. Gadsden State Community College
34. Grambling State University
35. H. Councill Trenholm State Technical College
36. Hampton University
37. Harris-Stowe State University
38. Hinds Community College
39. Howard University
40. Huston-Tillotson University
41. Interdenominational Theological College
42. J.F. Drake State Technical College
43. Jackson State University
44. Jarvis Christian College
45. Johnson C. Smith University
46. Kentucky State University
47. Knoxville College Δ
48. Lane College
49. Langston University
50. Lawson State Community College-Birmingham Campus
51. LeMoyne-Owen College
52. Lewis College of Business Δ
53. Lincoln University
54. Lincoln University of Pennsylvania
55. Livingstone College
56. Meharry Medical College
57. Miles College
58. Mississippi Valley State University
59. Morehouse College
60. Morehouse School of Medicine
61. Morgan State University
62. Morris Brown University Δ
63. Morris College
64. Norfolk State University
65. North Carolina A&T State University

66. North Carolina Central University
67. Oakwood College
68. Paine College
69. Paul Quinn College
70. Philander Smith College
71. Prairie View A&M University
72. Rust College
73. Saint Augustine's College
74. Saint Paul's College
75. Savannah State University
76. Selma University
77. Shaw university
78. Shelton State Community College-Fredd Campus
79. Simmons College of Kentucky Δ
80. Sojourner-Douglass College
81. South Carolina State University
82. Southern University and A&M College
83. Southern University at New Orleans
84. Southern University at Shreveport
85. Southwestern Christian College
86. Spelman College
87. St. Phillip's College
88. Stillman College
89. Talladega College
90. Tennessee State University
91. Texas College
92. Texas Southern University
93. Tougaloo College
94. Tuskegee University
95. University of Arkansas at Pine Bluff
96. University of Maryland Eastern Shore
97. University of the District of Columbia
98. University of the Virgin Islands
99. University of the Virgin Islands-Kingshill
100. Virginia State University

101. Virginia Union University
102. Virginia University of Lynchburg
103. Voorhees College
104. West Virginia State University
105. Wilberforce University
106. Wiley College
107. Winston-Salem State University
108. Xavier University of Louisiana

Δ At the time of this book's first publication, these institutions were no longer accredited.

www.ingramcontent.com/pod-product-compliance
Lightning Source LLC
Chambersburg PA
CBHW071201090426
42736CB00012B/2407